Enjoy a mystery date with your dog!

DATES IN THE STATES

A COUPLE TRAVELING THE UNITED STATES ON A BUDGET

I0541623

Mystery Doggie Date
Irondequoit, NY

By Dates in the States

"To all the dogs we've ever loved - this one's for you."

Dates in the States

Introduction

Hey there! We're Crystal and Shane, the duo behind Dates in the States, where we share our love for discovering unique adventures, unforgettable moments, and hidden gems across the U.S. Whether you're searching for a fun date idea, a new place to explore, or just a little inspiration, we've got you covered!

Our Mystery Date Books are designed to help couples (and adventurous friends!) shake up their routine and experience the best local spots in a fun, intentional way. Inside, you'll find a curated collection of date ideas—each one meant to be completed over the course of a single day in a specific neighborhood. All of which are a surprise until you flip the page!

We hope this book helps you laugh more, explore more, and connect more—with each other and with your city. Let the mystery begin!

Here's What To Expect:

Whether you're a local or just visiting, this date is all about spending quality time with your best four-legged friend while discovering some of Irondequoit's hidden gems.

Here's what's in store for your pup-tastic adventure:

Explore wooded trails, sandy shores, or lake paths at a local park. Kick back with craft beer and great food while your pup gets love from the staff at a favorite local brewery. Wrap up the day with ice cream—and don't forget a scoop of vanilla for your furry date!

Start

Durand Eastman Park/Beach

1342 Lakeshore Blvd
Rochester, NY 14622

Kick off your doggie date at Durand Eastman Park, a beautiful place where nature meets the shoreline of Lake Ontario. Choose your own adventure—walk along the paved path that hugs the beach, let your pup splash in the waves along the water, or take a sandy stroll across the beach itself. If you prefer a walk through in the woods, wander through the peaceful trails off Zoo Road, where the canopy of trees provides shade and a quiet escape. We also suggest exploring the paths near White Lady's Castle, where your pup can sniff out an adventure while you take in the eerie beauty of the old stone structure.

No matter which route you take, this stop is all about fresh air, wagging tails, and making memories with your best furry friend!

Second Stop

Irondequoit Beer Company

765 Titus Ave

Rochester, NY 14617

After your scenic adventure at Durand Eastman Park, head over to Irondequoit Beer Company for a well-earned refreshment and a delicious bite to eat. This local gem features a welcoming atmosphere, a fantastic selection of craft beers, and a spacious dog-friendly patio, perfect for kicking back with your pup by your side.

The staff here love dogs, so expect plenty of tail wags and extra pets for your furry companion. While you sip on a cold beverage of your choice, your pup can cool down with a fresh bowl of water. Feeling hungry? IBC also offers an amazing food menu, with a rotating selection of seasonal dishes that pair perfectly with their brews.

Third Stop

Don's Original

4900 Culver Rd
Rochester, NY 14622

No doggie date is complete without a sweet treat! After your meal at IBC, head to Don's Original for a scoop of their signature frozen custard. This beloved local spot features a convenient walk-up window and outdoor seating, perfect for enjoying your treat with your pup by your side.

Choose from creamy custard cones, thick milkshakes, or sundaes topped just the way you like. And of course, don't forget to share a little pup-friendly vanilla scoop with your furry date!

Third Stop Alternative

Bill Gray's

4870 Culver Rd

Rochester, NY 14622

If you're in the mood for something a little different, Bill Gray's is another great choice just steps away. Known for their classic soft-serve ice cream, they also offer a walk-up window and outdoor patio seating where your pup can relax while you indulge.

Grab a cone, a sundae, or a signature milkshake to wrap up your doggie adventure on a sweet note—and maybe let your pup sneak a lick of vanilla, too!

Final Stop

Irondequoit Bay Bridge & Lighthouse
5000 Culver Rd.
Rochester, NY 14622

If you're looking to walk off your meal and treats, consider a leisurely stroll around the Irondequoit Bay and Lighthouse area. This picturesque spot offers breathtaking views of the bay and the historic lighthouse. It's also a fantastic location for bird-watching, with opportunities to spot a variety of species. Our favorites are the bald eagles!

Enjoy the fresh lake air and make more memories with your furry companion as you take in the sights and sounds of this beautiful local gem.

Add Your Photos

Keepsakes

Keepsakes

Thank you for joining us on this dog-friendly mystery date adventure! We hope you and your pup had a blast exploring Irondequoit, NY, making memories, and sharing some special treats along the way.

But the fun doesn't stop here! Keep discovering exciting mystery dates in other cities by visiting DatesInTheStates.com, where you can grab physical and digital copies of our date books. Want more adventures? Join our Mystery Date Book Club to receive a brand-new mystery date every month!

We'd love to see your adventures—tag us in your date photos on social media for us to reshare! @datesinthestates

Check out some of our other Mystery Date Books:

Webster, NY – Lakeside charm, local eats, and small-town surprises perfect for a relaxing day out.

East Aurora, NY – A nostalgic escape featuring scenic trails, delightful shops, and a vintage movie night.

Hornell, NY – A hidden gem in the Finger Lakes region with art, nature, and charming local spots waiting to be discovered.

I Love ROC + Cats – Explore local art, sip coffee with adoptable cats, browse a charming bookstore, and end with a delicious downtown meal. Perfect for solo dates, friend hangouts, or cat-loving couples!

🗹 Shop them all at DatesInTheStates.com
📷 Tag your adventures: @datesinthestates

Your next date is only a page away.

The chalkboard sign reads: I LOVED HIM FIRST

About the Creators

Crystal, the writer and creator, is a storyteller at heart. When she's not uncovering hidden gems for the next date night idea, she runs her own digital marketing company, helping small businesses improve their content marketing, increase visibility in their communities, and streamline their online presence.
Visit: crystalstatskey.com

Shane, her husband and partner in adventure, is a dedicated personal trainer and the owner of Beekstar Fitness in Irondequoit, NY. He specializes in working with clients who have limited mobility, helping them build muscle and focus on pain areas so they can regain strength and confidence in their daily lives.
Visit: beekstarfitness.com

Crystal and Shane have explored every U.S. state except Alaska (coming soon!) and are now visiting countries in alphabetical order. Whether road-tripping or curating Mystery Date experiences, they're always chasing their next adventure.

Local Love

A few local gems in Irondequoit worth exploring on your next date.

UNION TAVERN

HAUNTED BAR RESTAURANT

4565 CULVER RD, IRONDEQUOIT, NY 14622

ANATOLIA MEDITERRANEAN GRILL

MIDDLE EASTERN CUISINE

4671 CULVER RD, ROCHESTER, NY 14622

SEA BREEZE BOWL

BOWLING ALLEY

4306 CULVER RD, ROCHESTER, NY 14622

Want to see your business here? See the next page for details on how to join!

Want to be featured?

MYSTERY DATE BOOK PACKAGES

—

Are you a small business looking to reach new customers? Feature your business in our next Mystery Date Book! Choose from our partnership packages below to connect with couples seeking unique experiences and exclusive deals.

Package One
LOCAL LOVE LISTING

—

A quick shoutout to show you're part of the neighborhood vibe.

Listed in the "Local Love" section of your designated neighborhood date book

Includes business name, address, and social link

Optional: Offer a small promo (e.g., 10% off for book holders)

1 social media shout-out when the book launches

$45

Package two
FEATURE STOP

—

You're not just a business— you're part of the experience.

Marked as a "Must-Stop" on a Mystery Date

Full-page feature in the book with your story, offerings and photo

Includes 1 social media feature — a dedicated post and story highlighting your business

Note: To ensure each feature is genuine and experience-based, we require a hosted visit prior to inclusion.

$95

Package three
PARTNER & SELLER

—

Be the spot and the source.

Everything in Tier 2

PLUS: Option to sell the Mystery Date Books at your location

Includes a bulk purchase of 10 books (yours to price + sell)

Keep 100% of the profits from in-store sales

Bonus: Tag as an official pickup location in our promotions

$150

Prices are subject to change

Feel free to reach us at any time by sending us an email to say hi and to learn more! We look forward to hearing from you.

| www.datesinthestates.com | datesinthestatesblog@gmail.com |

Sponsors & Affiliates

Our sponsors and affiliates help make our adventures possible! Explore the amazing brands and businesses that support our community.

Wanderful

Wanderful is a global community for women who love to travel. Connect, explore, and join a local hub near you!

Join our Book Club!

Join our Mystery Date Book Club and be part of a travel-inspired community, discovering unique local adventures together!

HomeExchange

HomeExchange lets you swap homes with travelers worldwide for authentic, affordable stays. Join today and travel differently!

Shop our books at a store near you!

Little Button Craft
658 South Ave.
Rochester, NY 14620

The Pawsitive Cat Cafe
120 East Ave. Ste 100
Rochester, NY 14604

Yesterday's Muse Books
32 West Main St.
Webster, NY 14580

Writers & Books
740 University Ave,
Rochester, NY 14607

Littleberger Florist
63 North Avenue,
Webster, NY 14580

Flight Wine Bar
262 Exchange Blvd,
Rochester, NY 14608

Scents by Design
728 University Ave,
Rochester, NY 14607

Union Tavern
4565 Culver Rd,
Irondequoit, NY 14622

DATES IN THE STATES

A COUPLE TRAVELING THE UNITED
STATES ON A BUDGET

Contact Us

datesinthestates.com

datesinthestatesblog@gmail.com

📍

Based in Rochester, NY

CONNECT WITH US ON SOCIAL!

@DATESINTHESTATES

_____